The Basics of Elevated Marketing Off the Grid

A Mini Handbook Introductory Guide
To Basic Non-linear Conscious Marketing
Concepts to Elevate Your Income & Impact

Alicia "WATERS"

Mike Martinez

For ordering, booking, permission, or questions, contact the author.
www.anwempires@gmail.com
www.amazon.com/author/alicianwaters

ISBN:13:978-1502368126

Printed in the United States of America by Create Space

The Basics of Elevated Marketing Off the Grid

Dedication & Acknowledgments

This is a general dedication to every current, future entrepreneur and conscious marketer who is committed to serving the masses with excellence, while making their desired income as they make an impact.

I give thanks and acknowledgments to God and to every mentor, coach and/or other marketers who have helped to elevated my marketing agenda.

I also acknowledge and give thanks to Mike Martinez for contributing his wisdom from the years of his dynamic marketing experience and expertise to this publication.

Table of Contents

The Basics of Elevated Marketing Off the Grid

Introduction: The Basics

Making daily decisions about best marketing practices can be challenging at times especially if you have already spent much of your time and resources trying to accomplish your marketing efforts.

Elevated Marketing Off the Grid is a mini handbook journal planner guide with concepts that aid and assist with aligning your marketing efforts for making wise investments of time and resources.

The primary goal of marketing your business or products is to be able to monetize your efforts through marketing while changing the lives of others through your offerings.

The overall concept of *Elevated* Marketing Off the Grid is about being a non-linear, intuitive, and an awakened marketer who partners with the energy of your conscious business and your bank account to provide you with insights about your marketing agenda.

Internet & Video Marketing Consultant Mike Martinez says; "I believe marketing should focus on three primary things; a) Targeting the ideal prospects, or target market. b) Have the ability to create mass exposure, through multiple mediums.

The Basics of Elevated Marketing Off the Grid

c) Provide the ideal solution to your audience in order to build know, like and trust. If these three things can be set in motion CONSISTENTLY, the rest grows at it's appropriate times." I agree with Mike.

Also, when it comes to the subject of marketing, I've found over the years that it's not about always following a simple step by step formula or linear format to bring the results that you desire. Sometimes you have to try a non-linear approach and use your current marketing efforts in a completely different way. Non-linear marketing often requires marketing in an arena that you've never considered.

Cross niche-marketing or sub-niche marketing involves expanding outside of your normal target audience to add value in new territories, gain more exposure and do something different than what is being done by other so called experts.

This awareness will help you to monetize your marketing from an awakened and elevated vantage point. This guide and journal planner is designed to inspire you to take your marketing efforts to the next levels through creating a more consistent off the grid structure for next level success.

This process allows you to formulate a plan to incorporate into your business agenda immediately and/or at another time.

The Basics of Elevated Marketing Off the Grid

Incorporating elevated consciousness into your marketing efforts will help to increase your impact and your income. It's time to co-create and up-level your agenda for monetizing your marketing efforts. The subject of higher consciousness is often linked with the spiritual aspects of embodying our inner divinity or our internal portal to access Universal Intelligence. This is where the organic true nature to operate from what most conscious entrepreneurs would call the "Higher Self", begins to emerge to provide us with an elevated perspective for how to proceed in our endeavors.

There is great power in using the concept of elevated consciousness within your marketing agenda. This concept allows you to market from a place of having ultimate connection to the voice of your tribe or target market to metaphysically know what to create for them and/or when and how to market your offerings. Being tapped into the deepest aspects of yourself and Universal Intelligence yields unfathomable results for you and those you serve. As mentioned previously, it's time for you to make a great impact to change your reality and others.

Multi-Niche Mini-Book Marketer
Alicia Nicole WATERS

The Basics of Elevated Marketing Off the Grid

Elevated Marketing Off the Grid 101

If you've ever observed a house that is off of the grid, it is lifted off of the traditional foundation and often allows you see underneath the actual framework. Elevated marketing off the grid can also be viewed in direct correlation to how elevation can provide us an opportunity to see what is really going on underneath our surface reality within our business and marketing agendas.

As our business frameworks evolve we begin changing the rules from the traditional concepts. This allows us to see that though we have a complete and stable framework with our plans for marketing, being elevated off of the grid allows us to have a more conscious perspective for our agenda to see other alternatives. Often, we are mostly looking head on and only being able to see through limited lens because we are so close to our normal strategic planning.

Great shifts occur when we learn how to market off the grid because every decision that you make is already being made from a higher perspective to create higher dreams for your life. Though marketing off the grid for a moment might feel like you have to surrender a current process that you're accustomed to, the results for how it re-aligns your marketing path is vibrationally undeniably one of the best game changers for creating a more expanded business than you've ever envisioned. So, I encourage you to explore coming off of the grid to market from a higher level.

The Basics of Elevated Marketing Off the Grid

Elevated Video Marketing

(Internet & Video Marketing Consultant Mike Martinez)

Elevated Marketing is about taking your marketing to the next level. Video marketing is one of the easiest ways to present your message to your audience in a creative, personal, and eloquent manner. Video marketing offers you four key advantages over other online media;

- Video messages are delivered and received at a higher conversion than any other media. Websites with sales message videos have statistically proven to convert much higher, as well as, retain visitors on the site longer than static sites.
- Video messages help to create a bond with your audience. Provided the video producer is honest and sincere, audiences quickly connect with messages that resonate with their concerns. This eventually creates the three elements needed for any sales success, Know, Like and Trust.
- Video messages that are designed to train on specific subjects are the fastest way to position yourself as an expert in your field. Again, provided that the video producer is honest, sincere, and providing value, the audience will grow rather quickly and with a certain sense of loyalty.
- Video marketing offers one of the easiest Search Engine Optimization (SEO) methods online.

The Basics of Elevated Marketing Off the Grid

SEO is constantly changing; however, video has maintained strength in search engines, and often offer the top results for searches.

Elevated Marketing Video Strategy

So how do you start using video to market your business? As simple as video marketing is, there are several steps that lead to mathematical success with video marketing. Many people simply get themselves in front of the camera and shoot video without having a clear-cut objective.

Scattered actions produce scatter results. Focused actions produce focused results. It behooves video marketers to prepare a well thought out plan before they stand in front of the camera. The key three questions to be answered before the recording starts are;

1. Who is my target audience? This question is the one most people neglect to answer, unrealistically thinking that their product or service fits a wider audience than it actually does. One of the key advantages of identifying a very specific target market prior to recording your video is that the marketer simplifies the entire process by being able to uncover and address problems and concerns related to the target market.

This will eloquently lead to the three elements of sales success we already addressed, when your audience knows, likes and trust you because you are offering solutions to their problems and concerns.

2. What is my message? Delivering your message is an art. It is not enough to simply identify the problems and concerns of your audience. The art comes from delivering a message that gets received properly. Language is very important here. The best way is to become a master at storytelling. Facts tell, stories sell. Again, it behooves the video producer to take some time and prepare a well thought out story that builds a bridge to their product or service. Use the story to connect your product or service as the solution to the audience's problems or concern.

3. What action do you want your video viewer to take? This is referred to as the call to action. What do you want to happen next? Sign up for the free report (list building)? Call me on the phone? Attend my next webinar? Subscribe to my YouTube channel? There are endless directions you can steer your audience. Put time into identifying where you want to take your viewers next. This final step will determine the ultimate outcome of your entire process.

In closing, I sincerely hope that you have gotten a glimpse into the importance of how video marketing fits into the Elevated Marketing discussed in this book. Ultimately, the key is to provide value. Video can be a great tool toward that means. If you get into the habit of providing outstanding value via video, before asking for the sale, your business will grow easily and effortlessly. Try it and the results will impress you.

Create Your 90 Day Marketing Road Map

Begin by creating three stages of a Conscious 30 Day Focus for Monetizing Your Marketing Efforts then rinse and repeat or up-level while transitioning into your next phase. (Create a plan, yet, always leave room for divine editing).

Here are 3 easy conscious stages to begin (these steps might seem very basic; however, it's about up-leveling the calibration of these basic frameworks).

Step 1: Having Elevated Clarity in The Present

Know what you want for your business now?

Write down how much money you desire to receive?

How many clients you want?

What are the benefits and results of this outcome?

What will it allow you to do more of?

The Basics of Elevated Marketing Off the Grid

Step 2: Create Your Elevated Planning Process

Co-create with your tribe energetically. Take some time out to get present with a journal and begin asking your tribe what is that they need right now, what will they pay you for right now and how you can create divine right exchange and value?

Allow them to create through you what they want instead of what you think that they need.

Create Your Next Level Attraction Magnet to Generate & Drive Traffic

Examples: Consider providing or developing a system of Higher Level offerings for higher level leads: consider offering a non-traditional training, VIP days, speaking, and/or create a community. Begin offering a series of relevant reports that aren't not just informational but transformational. Co-create with in Joint Ventures if necessary. Again, whatever your tribe requires.

Secondary Tip:

Consider: Sending out one email or create a video a week that is "Solutions Driven" that focuses on the benefits and next level results and not the process of your offering.

Your current clients and/or prospects will pre-qualify and/or convert themselves for your next level offerings.

Develop your intuitive time line and strategies

Step 3: Apply Elevated Execution

Implementation through right inspired actions of your co-creative planning process. Rinse, repeat and/or up-level for your next 30-day process.

The Basics of Elevated Marketing Off the Grid

Off the Grid Marketing Challenge:

Ask yourself a series of higher level questions around your marketing agenda.

Questions to Consider:

I'm curious to know how I can begin marketing with a non-linear approach?

I'm wondering how I can begin to raise my consciousness from a traditional approach to a more elevated marketing perspective?

Elevated Marketing Journaling & Planning Section

The Basics of Elevated Marketing Off the Grid

Elevated Marketing Insights & Planning

Establish your daily, weekly or monthly marketing
agenda/plan of action from the readings.

More Notes:

Elevated Marketing Insights & Planning

Establish your daily, weekly or monthly marketing
agenda/plan of action from the readings.

More Notes:

Elevated Marketing Insights & Planning

Establish your daily, weekly or monthly marketing agenda/plan of action from the readings.

More Notes:

Elevated Marketing Insights & Planning

Establish your daily, weekly or monthly marketing agenda/plan of action from the readings.

More Notes:

Elevated Marketing Insights & Planning

Establish your daily, weekly or monthly marketing agenda/plan of action from the readings.

The Basics of Elevated Marketing Off the Grid

More Notes:

Elevated Marketing Insights & Planning

Establish your daily, weekly or monthly marketing agenda/plan of action from the readings.

More Notes:

Elevated Marketing Insights & Planning

Establish your daily, weekly or monthly marketing agenda/plan of action from the readings.

More Notes:

Elevated Marketing Insights & Planning

Establish your daily, weekly or monthly marketing
agenda/plan of action from the readings.

More Notes:

Elevated Marketing Insights & Planning

Establish your daily, weekly or monthly marketing agenda/plan of action from the readings.

More Notes:

Elevated Marketing Insights & Planning

Establish your daily, weekly or monthly marketing agenda/plan of action from the readings.

More Notes:

Elevated Marketing Insights & Planning

Establish your daily, weekly or monthly marketing
agenda/plan of action from the readings.

More Notes:

Elevated Marketing Insights & Planning

Establish your daily, weekly or monthly marketing agenda/plan of action from the readings.

More Notes:

Elevated Marketing Insights & Planning

Establish your daily, weekly or monthly marketing
agenda/plan of action from the readings.

More Notes:

Elevated Marketing Insights & Planning

Establish your daily, weekly or monthly marketing agenda/plan of action from the readings.

More Notes:

Elevated Marketing Insights & Planning

Establish your daily, weekly or monthly marketing agenda/plan of action from the readings.

More Notes:

Elevated Marketing Insights & Planning

Establish your daily, weekly or monthly marketing
agenda/plan of action from the readings.

More Notes:

Write A Brief Summary About
Your Elevated Marketing Experience

The Basics of Elevated Marketing Off the Grid

Summary Continued:

The Basics of Elevated Marketing Off the Grid

Author's Information & Contributions

Alicia Nicole WATERS

Alicia "WATERS", the creator of the platform Marketing Mastery Marketplace. She is a multi-niche mini-book marketer, media marketing communications mentor and a published author of over 150 books.

Contributed to This Publication:

Introduction: The Basics

Elevated Marketing Off the Grid 101

Create Your 90 Day Marketing Road Map

Off the Grid Marketing Challenge

For More Marketing Resources visit:
www.marketingmasterymarketplace.blogspot.com

To Book the Author for speaking engagements email: anwempires@gmail.com

Author's Information & Contributions

Mike Martinez

Mike Martinez is a blogger, online marketing mentor and an expert video marketer. The creator of the "The Video Marketing Challenge," Mike has helped countless people go from novice video marketers to expert levels at break-neck speed.

Contributed to This Publication:

Elevated Video Marketing & Strategies

Mike's personal blog is www.mike-martinez.com and www.thevideomarketingchallenge.com.

Mike can be found on Facebook at www.facebook.com/onlinemarketingmentor

The Basics of Elevated Marketing Off the Grid

For Continued Learning & Advancement

Visit:
www.marketingmasterymarketplace.blogspot.com

Also, if you enjoyed this resource, please
consider writing a review on Amazon.com

Thanks & Blessings